Non-fiction Writing Essentials: A Writer's Toolkit

Contents

Introduction

This book is for non-fiction writers who are new to writing and for those with experience who feel they are in a rut and need a new perspective. Using simple language, this book focuses on giving writers a toolbox of skills to enable them to write really good non-fiction books. Whether you're writing 'how-to' guides, instructional manuals, technical journals, text books, or travel guides, this book will help take your writing skills to the next level. It includes many effective writing strategies that can help you craft a clear and concise message, while creating interest and improving understanding for your readers.

As a tertiary level lecturer for over 20 years and a Number One selling Amazon Kindle author, I rarely got what I wanted from other 'how to write' authors. My view is that if you want to write great quality non-fiction that satisfies your readers, you need to know something about how learners learn. In other words, writers need to be able to deliver a message with clarity and in an interesting manner. When your readers become engaged with your books, you know you're writing good books.

As a non-fiction writer, you can craft an extremely effective message by using some very simple, yet incredibly powerful, principles that can be used as a blue-print for every non-fiction book you write. Employ the right principles in your writing and you'll start creating great quality content that really satisfies.

Lastly, this book is an example of the principles within. I continue to use all of the principles and methods in this book in my own writing; both in academic writing and non-fiction. I hope this book leaves you feeling enthusiastic, motivated, and empowered with your own non-fiction writing.

I sincerely hope you enjoy the read. Let's move on.

About the Author

Amos is a lecturer at Unitec Institute of Technology in Auckland, New Zealand where he's been lecturing at a tertiary level for over 20 years in the area of commercial construction methodology and architectural draughting. He has a deep interest in the practice of learning and teaching and the use of eLearning technologies. Amos is also a musician, songwriter, recording engineer, and producer, working in the music industry for over two decades. He's worked extensively in live sound and as a bass player/vocalist in working bands that have gigged around the world. He holds a Diploma in Audio Engineering from SAE, a Graduate Diploma in Higher Education and currently runs sHOWpONY, a boutique recording and production studio in Auckland, New Zealand.

Amos is also a prolific writer of non-fiction in the area of music production, arrangement, and mix engineering.

Please feel free to contact him by email at **show.pony@live.com**

Top-down Planning

Identify your goals, decide on your outcomes, and map out the topics of your book before you start writing

---

Author's note:
The idea of starting a book at the beginning and simply steaming ahead until the end never worked for me. Most of my writing has been non-fiction and a lot of it, learning material. This 'linear-sequential' approach always had me meandering off as I became distracted by interesting, but not always poignant, ideas along the way. A top-down planning method allowed me an over-arching view of my entire book and helped relieve the dreaded 'writer's block'. I went from, "where do I start, what shall I write first?" to formulating all my book's topics before I started writing a single word.

What is Top-down planning?

This is a really simple and powerful method for planning all the topics in your book before you start writing. The method requires you to explore all the most important aspects of the themes and issues while thinking about what your readers need to know most. It is a holistic approach that explores the book's content in general terms before the writing starts.

The 'Top-down' method is unintuitive because you design your book backwards

---

Why the Top-down planning method is effective

Even the best of us get tangled up in problems that cause our writing mojo to take a vacation. What if we had a method of writing that virtually said goodbye to that issue? If you're a struggling writer, or just starting out, it's common to run into problems like not knowing where to start and getting 'stuck' during the writing process. Even if you know your topic well, the sheer magnitude of your knowledge and experience can slow you down or paralyse you into inactivity.

Top-down planning is like brain-storming. When we brain-storm, we sketch or write ideas about our book's content. We think about the critical topics (chapters) and these topics help generate ideas to write about. We might get ideas for diagrams and images to improve clarity. We might think about other things, like the best sequence to develop our readers' understanding and how they could apply their new knowledge. In comparison, a linear-sequential approach has a writer starting at the beginning and attempting to write the book from start to finish. They must anticipate the content as they go, often back-tracking to revise, add or remove content due to duplication or omissions.

The Top-down approach saves time because:
1. You are more likely to cover the essential topics
Your time and energy are spent focusing on important information, rather than simply trying to generate written content.

2. It helps writer's-block
Top-down planning doesn't rely on your ability to be a writer, but requires you to be a planner. It's easier to think of all the important things to write about (planning) than it is to start writing about them.

3. It's faster and more accurate
Writing without planning makes it super easy to get off the topic. By writing to topics and key-words/key-phrases you give yourself a target to aim for.

How to do Top-down planning

1. Define the overall goal of your book
What are you trying to achieve with your book? Are you providing general information about a topic or a practical guide? Who is your target audience and what type of language or 'narrative' should you use to suit their needs?

2. Create your important topics
These are the most important topics that will be covered in your book – they become your chapters. You also need to consider what your readers may already want to know about your topic. Search your topic at websites like yahoo.answers.com and reddit.com to find this information.

3. Create keywords and key-phrases from your important topics
Develop ideas around your important topics by creating keywords and key-phrases that you want to explore under each topic. This step is about quickly capturing ideas which you will further develop when you start writing.

4. Create summary points
These are the key points that you want your readers to go away with after they finish reading this chapter. Creating these before you start writing is an effective way to help you keep your writing on target. For your readers, it distils complex discussion down into essential points and adds clarity at the end of a chapter.
Note: sometimes it works to swap around steps 3 and 4. In other words, create your summary points first, and then develop your keywords/phrases.

5. Start writing

Start writing the first things that come in to your head under each keyword and key-phrase. Don't worry about getting your spelling and grammar right; just start writing. For this step, the important thing is to capture more detailed ideas. You can do your proof-reading later. Methodically use this approach for each of the topics in your book. I like to use the 5 W's and an H approach (see later chapter) because it helps focus my writing and enables me to 'chunk' the information in a logical order.

6. Re-organise your content

Re-structure what you've written in step 5 so that the content flows in a logical and meaningful way for your readers. Check that your writing isn't too 'wordy' as this can create confusion for your readers.

The topics of proof-reading and editing have been purposely missed here and are covered in later chapters.

Summary

1. Top-down planning provides a broad overview of the finished product before you even start writing.

2. Top-down planning is more than simply considering the topics; it considers formatting, presentation, cover design, topics, narrative style, target audience and more.

3. Top-down planning is a faster and more accurate way to write because it helps you to target the essential topics before you writing.

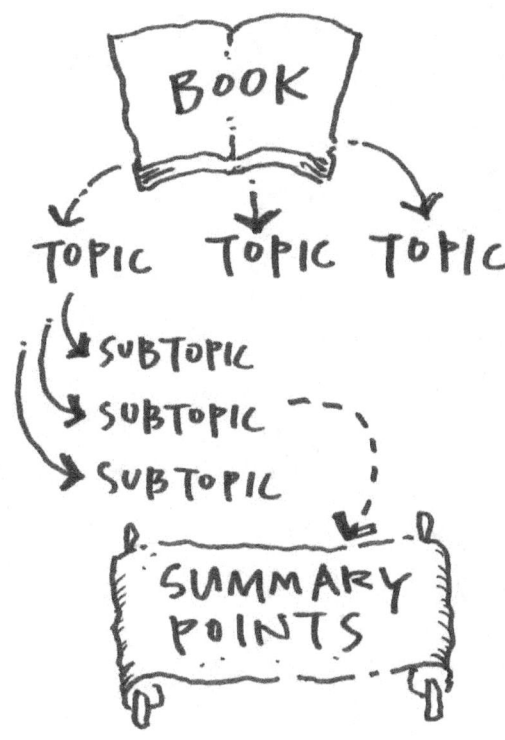

Image A – Topics lead to sub-topics, each with a summary

Outcomes

Outcomes provide clear goals for writers and clear expectations for readers

---

Author's note:
Writing outcomes is something I picked up in my early days as a lecturer writing student-learning materials. Once I got into the habit of firming up simple but clear outcomes BEFORE I started writing, they became my 'guiding light' for everything I wrote about. If you take this step seriously and get it right, your reasons for writing become clear and directed.

What are Outcomes?

An outcome is an explanation of the achievement expectations from a progression of learning. When we write a good outcome, we create a target for our writing that guides our entire approach. Outcomes can be simple or complex. They can state one goal or many. You don't need to include your outcome statements in your book but it can be very useful to re-word them and include them in your introduction section. Doing this gives readers absolute certainty about what they are going to learn from reading your book.

Outcomes should clearly state what your reader will be able to do after they have read your book. Outcomes guide writers toward crafting a powerful and succinct message with a purpose. They should be written carefully so that they capture the true essence of your goals and intentions. Outcomes enable writers to stick to what's important and ignore the rest. They are not just a target for the content of each chapter, but also a target for your entire book.

Because of this, outcomes need to be both broad AND concise. When you write your next book, think carefully about your outcomes; write them down, stick them on the wall, and refer to them often while you write.

> *Outcomes should clearly state what your reader will be able to do after they have read your book*

Why using Outcomes is an effective writing strategy

In education, it's common practice for teachers to design their outcomes for the courses before they start teaching and before any of the learning material is created. When writing non-fiction, writers need to know the knowledge and skills they expect their readers to gain by the end of the book. Creating proper outcomes is not a quick verbal summary one does in their head to validate their efforts. Rather, it's a methodical and considered process based on good practice. Outcomes should include an element of application that dictates the depth of learning. In other words, we describe what the learner can do with their new knowledge and skills.

An example of an outcome for construction students:

"At the end of this topic, students will be able to <u>identify</u> important features of commercial concrete construction".

The key word here is 'identify', and this outcome states that when students have finished studying this topic, they will be able to recognise and point their finger at some important aspects of a large concrete building. So that's great, but it's not a very deep learning experience. It is, however, part of a stair-casing approach to teaching, where learners learn the basics first, before moving on to more complex knowledge later. With this in mind, the teacher can add more Outcomes with a deeper learning expectation.

Let's look at an outcome with a deeper learning expectation:

"At the end of this topic, students will be able to <u>analyse</u> and <u>create</u> solutions to complex problems relating to commercial concrete construction".

Now this is higher level stuff. We're not asking students to point and nod, we're expecting them to examine problems and then use their new knowledge to come up with a reasonable solution.

So how does this help us as non-fiction writers?

When writers clearly define the intended Outcomes of their writing, they can target their writing clearly toward achieving their Outcomes.

*Outcomes should be clear and state
what your reader will be able to do
after they have read your book*

How to write Outcomes

Firstly, we decide on the Outcomes of our book <u>before</u> we start writing. Next, we use a prescribed way of writing them using descriptive verbs that state clearly what we expect the learner can do after completing the book. Remember that Outcomes are a planning tool and would not necessarily be explicitly included in your book.

The key to writing effective Outcomes is a two-part process.

Step one:
Start every outcome with the statement, 'At the end of this book readers will be able to (add a verb here)'. By doing this you focus clearly on what the reader will be able to do with their new-found knowledge once they've finished your book.

Here are some example verbs you can use (there are many more):

Adjust, analyse, apply, assemble, build, calculate, convert, compose, create, describe, design, discuss, draw, identify, manage, modify, navigate, plan, sketch, solve, summarise, supervise, write...and so on.

Step two:
Consider what Elements are required to support each Outcome. In the example below, there is one Outcome with 10 Elements. Each Element is potentially the title for each chapter in your book.

At the end of this book readers will be able to:

Apply principles of effective non-fiction writing by <u>planning</u> and <u>writing</u> a non-fiction book on a chosen topic. Evidence will be verified by demonstrating the following Elements in the finished book:

Elements for planning

1. Learning Outcomes are clearly described and relate to the overall book topic

2. Top-down planning is used to identify the main chapters and chapter topics

3. The TODS and SEE methods are used to help ensure that the content is covered clearly

Elements for writing

1. Written content aligns with the learning Outcomes

2. The author has written in a narrative suitable for the reader

3. Formatting and presentation is consistent and visually appealing

Summary

1. Outcomes serve as a goal for the writer and as expectations for the reader.

2. Always write your Outcomes before you start writing your book.

3. Outcomes don't need to be complex. Complex Outcomes often result in bigger, more complex books.

4. Take the time to write proper Outcomes that focus on what your reader will be able to do by the time they have finished your book. Use verbs such as: apply, explain, describe, identify, repair, discuss, illustrate, operate, demonstrate, assemble, construct, activate, etc.

Image B – What is the main aim of your book?

5 W's and an H

A method for ensuring writers include all the important and relevant information about their subject matter

---

Author's note:
My brilliant wife (a seasoned and sensible teacher) explained this principle to me many years ago. I often found myself in deep discussion with her about best principles in teaching, and in this instance, how to articulate new concepts to students in a clear and unambiguous way. The 5 W's and an H was a revelation to me and I instantly incorporated them into my lecturing. It's a technique that's now embedded in my thinking whenever I construct learning material or write books. I love it because it's so insanely simple in the way it can help writers dissect complex topics into simple questions. If this is the first time you've seen this, then I sincerely hope it provides the same value for you, that I experienced so long ago.

What is the 5 W's and an H method?

The 5 W's and an H method is a simple and powerful way to ensure you write about the important aspects of your topic. As a writer, you ask yourself about essential questions then you proceed to answer them. Writing the answers to these questions creates the content for your book. It doesn't matter if the topic is familiar or new to the writer because the simple prompting questions about 'what', 'why', 'how,' etc. guide the writer on a search-and-find mission.

So often, books miss one or more of these components, leaving readers with an incomplete understanding about a subject. When writers ask themselves the 5 W's and an H questions, they can provide their readers with breadth and depth about the subject matter. Writers can use this method to create simple or complex learning material depending on how many 5 W's and an H questions they ask.

The 5 W's and an H:
A simple and powerful method for ensuring you
cover all the important aspects of any topic

Why the 5 W's and an H method is so effective

Great questions lead to great answers. When you create great answers, you create great content for your book. When writers ask themselves questions like, "what are the most important things my readers need to know and why?" they have a prompt for providing a valuable and complete information package for their readers.

If you are a knowledge expert in your area, you may feel this method is not necessary because of your deep understanding. But what this method does is dissect your knowledge into concise packages of information that readers want to know about. Whether your knowledge area is fine arts, motorcycle maintenance or cooking, your readers still have the same questions. They still want to know what it is, why it's important, where it fits, who is involved, how it works, and so on.

When writers ask themselves these questions, they create a checklist for the content they need to create for their book. When writers ask the right questions, they can write about the things their readers want and need to know.

The 5 W's and an H provide focusing questions for writers to answer, and in answering, we create the content for our book

How the 5 W's and an H works

The matter of how detailed your readers' understanding will be, depends on what questions you ask under each one of these categories. The 5 W's and an H method prompts writers to examine the key questions that readers need to know about the book's subject matter. This is a critical step in the construction of the book because it reveals the key aspects of the things our readers need to know about a topic.

In this book, each chapter follows the same structure, where the main written content consists of 'what', 'why', and 'how'. I decided to omit the 'when/where/who' because I felt they didn't warrant a separate section, but were better embedded within the first three categories.

Sometimes you'll find that you don't need to include all the 'Ws', but in almost every case, you need to cover the 'How', the 'What' and the 'Why'. A good approach is to ask yourself as many questions as possible under each category, then select the relevant ones to write about.

Finally, don't under estimate the power and value of this method. As writers, our passion and impatience can get the better of us, leading us to skip important planning steps like this. The good news is that it doesn't take long to come up with a fairly broad list of topics using the 5 W's and an H method.

Example questions using the 5 W's and an H method

What
What is it? What is the point? What are the advantages/disadvantages? What is important/not important? What is it used for? What is good/bad? What does it look/sound/feel like? What happened/didn't happen? What is the best way/worst way to do it? What can you expect to gain/lose?

Why
Why is it /useful/good/bad? Why is it important/not important? Why do this/not do this? Why do it this way? Why does it work this way or feel like this? Why is this method important/critical/useful/not useful? Why is it dangerous? Why is it an advantage/disadvantage?

Who
Who is involved/not involved? Who does what? Who are the stakeholders? Who was there? Who is/was responsible/not responsible? Who is the most important person? Who is the leader? Who are the followers?

Where
Where does/did it happen geographically? (In a room? In a laboratory? On a building site? In another country?) Where can it be found? Where can you do this/not do this?

When

When does/did it happen? What year/month/week/day/time? When is the right time/wrong time? When does it fit into the entire process?

How

How does it work? How is it done? How is it done best? How does it fit in with other things in the process? How did it happen?

These are just some of the questions you can ask. You will come up with more relevant and specific questions related to your topic.

Summary

1. The 5 W's and an H create focusing questions to prompt writers to cover the important content for the chapters in their books.

2. The 5 W's and an H outlines the <u>breadth</u> of topics to cover. The <u>depth</u> of each topic depends on the number of what/why/how/when/where/who questions asked.

3. Don't under-estimate the power and value of this important planning step. Do it before you start writing the detailed content in your book.

Image C – The 5 W's and an H

Narrative Style

Craft and pitch a clear message at the right level for your intended audience

---

Author's note:
My experience is that some authors may be unaware of the particular narrative style they use, while for others, it becomes their signature that they hone and develop. Where some styles are conversational, others are crisp and formal. Some impart humour at every turn, where others are descriptive and colourful. Whatever your style, having an awareness of how this fits with your intended audience will help you deliver an effective message to your readers. You may decide to develop one style or you may need to have a few styles depending on the types of books you write. Personally, I love to pick up a book with a flowing and easy-going narrative peppered with humour and interesting snippets.

What is a narrative style?

A narrative style is the writing technique used by the author. While it is very much about how an author structures information and conveys ideas, it is more about how they add 'personality' to their writing. The idea of personality relates to how the author embellishes and injects style into their writing.

Let's consider a hypothetical book about how to grow indoor plants. This book is based around a list of 25 important points critical to successfully growing plants indoors. In isolation, the 25 points are a rather 'dry' and an unappetising collection of facts. The author adds personality to these facts by using an easy-going conversational style of writing, setting the reader at ease. Perhaps the author adds a little humour by including anecdotes to enhance the facts. The author purposely limits the botanical jargon so that the book appeals to a wider audience. In this example, the author is sensitive to the needs of the target audience and fashions a narrative style to suit.

The type of language you use in any book is directly related to the book's genre and your audience. The right narrative style connects your readers with your book, while the wrong style disengages them. It's critical to get your language right for your genre because it can affect the accessibility and credibility of your book. In our 'how to grow indoor plants' example above, limiting the jargon means the readers wouldn't be continuously tripping up over big, unpronounceable words. However, to a professional, this book may have more appeal if it included just the facts along with all the colourful botanical nomenclature.

When a book has an accessible narrative style, the reader can engage in the written content more easily. Therefore, it's critical that an author understands their audience and fashions their content accordingly.

Author credibility

Author credibility relates to the reader's belief in the relevance and quality of the message. For example, if a specialised book about music production uses a lot of slang and is mostly void of technical language common to that topic, readers may feel that the writer lacks experience and knowledge on the topic.

Important components in a narrative style:

1. Writing in the first or third person.

2. Using humour, stories, and facts as a way to add 'personality' to the narrative.

3. The use of slang, jargon, and colloquialisms.

4. A free-flowing conversational vs rigid-instructional style.

5. Tense: past or present.

6. Viewpoint: Impartial or biased.

7. And many more, such as the use of simile, metaphor, and hyperbole.

The right narrative style connects your readers with your book, while the wrong style disengages them

Why is narrative style important?

When we consider our target audience we need to know things like their language, gender, age, experience, and education. Then we need to write in a way that complements these factors. For example, readers with English as a second language struggle with jargon, slang, clichés and colloquialisms. Children (depending on their age) need language that allows them to understand the ideas; big words and complex discussions can be confusing for young readers. If you need to get further examples, try reading successful books by other authors in your genre. How do they write successfully for their target audience?

When we write children's books, we write for specific age groups. If it's ages 1 – 3, the stories are short with lots of pictures and VERY simple stories and a strong plot. Our readers don't have a long attention span and the images tell the story more than the words because pictures are what these young readers connect with (and of course, someone else is doing the reading for them!).

When we write learning material for young teens, we try to be as unambiguous as possible, introducing ideas and building on concepts logically. We're likely to use more formal language. We limit our use of complex terminology and jargon, or we explain it clearly. We're clear about our learners' prior knowledge and where this learning material fits in. We put ideas into context by providing examples. We get our students to demonstrate their understanding by putting theory into practice. There is a clear goal for our learners to attain a minimum understanding or a particular skillset by the end of the book.

When we write a biography, there is the freedom to tell the story the way we want. Precision is required; historic events need to be documented accurately. The goal of such a book is not usually to provide new skills, but to provide entertainment and insight into a person's life.

When we write a technical repair or maintenance manual, the goal is specific; to guide another person to successfully diagnose, repair, or upgrade a device of some sort. We're listing a series of actions to achieve a defined result. Often, such manuals will contain significant terminology, abbreviations, acronyms and diagrams. They also commonly assume a level of prior knowledge which the reader must have to navigate and use the manual usefully.

Example: different narrative styles on the topic of a beginner's guide to purchasing a guitar

ESOL (English for Speakers of Other Languages)
In this example we use simple language and keep the instructions clear and simple.

"Make sure you select your new acoustic guitar with the help of a professional. It is best to know your budget before you go shopping. You also need to know the style of music you wish to play as this will help you choose the best guitar. The two most common types of acoustic guitars are steel-string and nylon-string."

Formal
In this example, we get more complex with the instructions and guidance

"When selecting your new guitar, ensure you get guidance from a professional guitarist. Although retailers can be helpful in the selection process, a professional player can provide more detailed advice regarding construction, tone, and best value for money. The 'string action' (height of the strings above the fret board) and guitar type (classical or steel) are significant factors affecting comfort and playability. Another consideration is the inclusion of a pickup. While this adds further cost, it allows the player to amplify the guitar for live playing."

Conversational
In this example we use a 'blog type' narrative style which is less formal with a friendlier tone.

"Basically, the best way to shop for a new acoustic guitar is to surf the Net and check out the brands and reviews of guitars in your price range. Cross pollinate this with a browse through your local music shop's website as not all models are available from all sellers. Don't buy someone else's second-hand crud unless you can try it out first. Even better, bring someone with you who knows what they're looking for. If you're buying new, then take all creative sales pitches with a pinch of salt; remember, salespeople are there to sell guitars and you're there to get something you still want to play in three years' time! A couple of years back, I was in our local music shop looking for a steel string acoustic and after a half hour conversation, discovered the assistant, who was new to the job, could talk the lingo but had never even played! Best advice – do your research and take your time, unless you like buying lots of guitars"!

Knowing your audience is critical to ensuring your writing style is engaging, relevant, and of value to your readers

Writers may find it useful to ask themselves questions like:

1. Why do I write the way I do?

2. Who am I trying to be to my readers?

3. What is my 'author personality' and how important is it to me and my readers?

4. Is my narrative style suitable and appropriate for my intended audience?

5. Could I improve my writing style so that my readers enjoy my books more? If so, how?

6. Do I need to get better educated to write about my topic?

Summary

1. Fashion your narrative style to suit your audience's age, experience, language and ability – know your 'author personality'.

2. Be clear about the intended outcome of your book. Is it a technical guide, a repair manual, or an expression of ideas?

3. Use jargon and technical language carefully. If you're unsure about your readers' understanding, then provide a glossary.

4. Know your readers' existing level of understanding and write appropriately.

Image D – What will satisfy your audience's appetite?

Crafting a Clear Message

Create your content with clarity

Author's note:
This technique is one that I finally 'found' after spending years being dissatisfied in how I was constructing written content for my tertiary level students. My students seemed to enjoy the learning material more when they knew where it was going before they started. In other words, they didn't like a linear sequential approach of drip-fed narrative which only clarified the direction of the learning material when they were well into it. They told me this, in slightly different words! However, it made lots of sense. This chapter comprises my own findings and strategy for structuring the information-flow with clarity. I hope you find it as revealing and as useful as I did.

What does it mean to craft a clear message?

Crafting a clear message allows our readers to get the maximum amount of information in the minimum amount of reading time. It also means writing in a way that gets to the point and doesn't confuse our readers. It also provides a pleasant reading experience; engaging the reader and assisting in their comprehension of the topic. A clear message is not only written clearly, but structured in a concise format.

However, it's one thing to explain what a clearly crafted message is and entirely another to do it. This chapter explains common pitfalls and effective methods to help you improve your own non-fiction writing. It also explains methods for structuring your writing in a logical way that will help your readers assimilate and understand the content.

---

*Readers get the big picture up front
and a contextualised message
before they dig in to the detail*

Why is message clarity important?

Verbiage, Circumlocution, and Waffle

There's some debate about who wrote "Excuse the long letter; I didn't have time to write a shorter one". However, the quote highlights a common problem with some writers; they write too much and in doing so, confuse the reader.

Some different words for waffle:
Circumlocution, longwinded-ness, redundancy, tautology, verbiage, verbosity.

The problem with waffle is that readers get distracted from the true essence of the message because of the unnecessary and extraneous content. What readers don't need is a diluted and meandering message that 'beats around the bush'. While waffle can be used successfully for comic effect (such as fiction, blogging and satire) it's best avoided for non-fiction.

The problem with writing too much about a topic is that:
1. It confuses readers by obscuring the true meaning of the message.

2. It can make something ordinary seem profound (sometimes an advantage!).

3. It takes longer to read.

Examples
Let's look at two examples. The first is concise and the second is the waffle:

Concise example:
The committee realised the team was acting illegally.

Waffle example:
It came to the committee's attention, in an unusual and unexpected way, that the team was, with complete disregard for the club, and under its own latitude, indulging in felonious activities.

The problem with waffle is that readers can get distracted from the message

While waffle is generally to be avoided in non-fiction writing, sometimes a verbose style can add interest if it's in the form of an interesting story or humorous experience. However, in non-fiction writing it's worthwhile to separate the waffle from the instructional part of your message. One way to do this is in the form of an 'author's note' (as used in this book) or introductory story which is visually separated from other content on the page. This separation allows the writer to use a different style that doesn't 'muddy' the main message.

The TODS Method

The TODS Method is a way of structuring your book's chapters to make them clearer for your readers. It's effective because readers get an overview of the content early and get more detail as it progresses. Finally, readers are given a summary of the content to help them understand the key points. Using this method consistently for each chapter will result in a clear and concise style that your readers will appreciate.

TODS is an acronym for:
1. Title
2. Overview
3. Detail
4. Summary

Title
A clear and concise Title is important because it quickly and clearly describes the content that follows. Avoid ambiguous and lengthy Titles because they can be confusing - short and sweet is the goal. Ensure that the visual formatting (font and size) is consistent for all Titles in your book. If they appear different they can confuse the reader because bigger and bolder text appears more important than smaller and un-bolded text.

Overview

The Overview is a VERY brief outline of the entire chapter and at best, is no more than a sentence or two. Your goal is to distil your message with economy and clarity. A well-written Overview prepares the reader for the upcoming information by briefly describing what they are about to read. It saves them time because they know early on, if the information is worth reading. Use a consistent font style for all chapter Overviews but use a font that is different from the Title and the Detail (main body) of your writing so that there is visual differentiation. In this book, the Overview has been written in italics.

Detail

This is the main body of your writing. It includes writing and images (photos, graphs, diagrams, sketches, cartoons, etc.). If you're writing an eBook then it can include multimedia (audio and video etc.). These are your conversations, explorations, claims, and more. Avoid a continuous monologue of unbroken text by using paragraphs. Use bold Titles to introduce new chunks of content. For maximum clarity, use the SEE Method (see below).

Summary

The Summary captures the key points from the content in your Detail section. If your Detail is long, then the Summary is a perfect way to remind your readers of what's important at the end. When learners are new to a topic, they can find it difficult to know what is important in the Detail. By summarising, you remove the difficulty and add the clarity they need. If your book is written in a way where each chapter builds on the previous and prepares them for the next, providing a Summary becomes extremely useful for the reader.

Create a clear and unambiguous message for your readers by using the TODS method

The SEE Method

This is a very effective method to help writers create concise and clear written content. It was developed by Dr Linda Elda and Dr Richard Paul. It works on the basis that every _statement_ made is followed by an _explanation_ and then an _example_. It results in a very clear way of writing.

Statement – Explanation – Example

You can use the SEE Method effectively by including it in the 'Detail' section (refer to the TODS Method) for each chapter. In other words, you write your content by making a statement, explaining it, and then giving an example. You repeat this pattern over and over until, hey presto, you've written a chapter. This method of writing creates a clear and consistent reading experience where each idea (statement) is explored, justified and supported with examples. When you combine the SEE Method of writing with the TODS Method for structuring your content, you create quality content in a logical order for your readers.

An example using SEE on the topic of hit songs:
(Statement)
At the time of writing (2015) more hit songs were written in the 90's than any other decade before or after.

(Explanation)
This was partly due to the availability of technology; basically, more people owned a radio in the 90's than ever before. However, the main reason for the peak of radio hits was due to the increase of new music genres. Prior to the 90's, one could count the number of popular music genres on one hand: rock, country, jazz, disco and pop.

(Example)
The popular London radio station EzyBeatsFM funded a study in 2007 that showed no fewer than 23 popular musical genres. Their benchmark for 'a popular musical genre' was based on music sales, supporting radio stations and listener surveys.

Glossary

A glossary is very useful because it provides an easily accessible list of specialised words and terms, and their explanations, relative to a specific area of knowledge. Glossaries are essential for books with complex terminology, or for readers who are new to a topic and may be confused about the meanings of words. Even for readers familiar with the knowledge, a glossary provides a useful way for them to quickly check the meaning of a word or phrase. For readers who have English as a second language, it further supports their understanding in the event they may simply be struggling with the language on a more general level.
. Breaking down the barrier of misunderstanding around jargon and specialist terms can be incredibly liberating for readers of all ages, ethnicity, gender and experience. This alone can render a book more suitable and saleable for a wider audience.

Key things to remember with a glossary:
1. Maintain alphabetical order with your terms

2. Terms can be either a word or phrases

3. A glossary is most useful when it has clear and concise

explanations

4. Glossary entries can be further enhanced by including short

examples

Summary

1. The TODS Method creates a logical hierarchical structure where the content of a topic is described early on and the main detail is summarised. TODS stands for Topic, Overview, Detail and Summary.

2. The SEE Method provides a simple and effective way for writers to create concise and clear written content, where the writer makes a Statement, gives an Explanation, then provides an Example.

3. Combining the TODS and the SEE methods can produce a very effective technique for delivering concise and well-explained written content.

4. Avoid waffle OR use it with care: keep your message clear and simple.

5. A glossary will provide further clarity around specialised terminology and can make your book more accessible for a wider range of diverse readers.

Image E – Which tools are best for the job?

Formatting

Organise your layout and content visually for maximum impact

Author's note:
In my experience, good formatting can 'make or break' a book. A great format can ooze professionalism. Readers are often unconsciously aware of how a good layout helps provide a pleasant reading experience. My own readers tend to find the content more appealing and engaging when it looks good – at least that's what they say! For me, formatting is something I do at the end of writing my book because it allows me to concentrate on the writing first, then the look and feel later.

What does good formatting look like?

Formatting is about how content (text and graphics) looks and is arranged on the page. A well-formatted book would have a consistent theme that would apply to all pages in your book. The layout of text would focus on the position of text on the page, such as page titles, sub-titles, main content, image references, page numbers and more. Good formatting would have images and diagrams of a similar size, positioned in the same place on the page. In both these examples, the layout of text and graphics would be the same for each chapter so that the book maintains a consistent visual theme. However, a book can have a good format but be poorly designed so it's critical that writers pay attention to both format and design (see Style Guide below).

A word of warning

It is difficult to control the formatting for eBook reading devices because eReaders often automatically control the font size and style, making a consistent page layout almost impossible to achieve. Some eReader devices default to certain fonts regardless of the font you have used in your original book. This will require you to format your book differently depending on the final publishing format. You will have far more control of your book's presentation in printed format, as an online book, and as a PDF, and far less with Amazon Kindle.

Good looking content presents a perception of quality

Why is formatting important?

A well-organised and consistent layout provides reader confidence because readers know what to expect as they progress through the book. For example, if all chapters start with a descriptive overview and end with a summary, it provides readers with a confident expectation for upcoming content. Consistent formatting also allows readers to navigate and find content easily due to its position and appearance. For example, you might create a bold outline around every summary section so that readers can easily see the summaries when flicking through the book.

When text and graphics are arranged well on the page, with plenty of white space between them, it becomes easier on the eye because there is less density of information on the page. Adding space between chunks of information allows ideas to be separately presented – it's almost like allowing your reader to have a short break before moving on to the next piece of information. Reader confusion can result if too many ideas are condensed in the same visual space on the page. In the same way that a fine restaurant gives attention to the visual presentation of food on the plate, writers need to ensure their content is presented in a similarly pleasing manner.

While formatting deals with the organisation and arrangement of the content on the page, design is about how things look both individually and in combination with each other. More specifically, design relates to colour choice, backgrounds, infographics, font style, diagrams, images and more. A good design coupled with good formatting enables writers to create pleasing visual themes for their books.

A good Style Guide can reinforce
the theme of your book

The Style Guide

A Style Guide is like a way to bring design and formatting together. It works like a collection of rules that apply to how the content in your book is arranged and presented. If you feel confident you can create your own Style Guide, otherwise, you can get a designer to create one for you. Style Guides can be in printed or electronic format, such as a PDF.

Style Guides are available in varying formats and are usually designed specifically to suit a type of publication. For example, a travel agency might have a Style Guide that applies to all their brochures and travel guides. From educational institutions to finance consultants: all have their own needs in how their publications look and feel relative to their audience. Ideally, the same requirements would apply to the Style Guide used for your non-fiction books. This is important because the visual themes should support the information theme.

How visual themes support information
If your book is about IT then the visual theme would ideally be 'high tech'. From a design aspect, earthy colours might be avoided. A very modern style of font would ideally be used for all text. Graphical cues may be used such as electronic components in the chapter headings and under the page numbers. Overall, the intention would be to create a technological visual theme that supports the information in the book.

Considering the above example, what could the visual theme be for a book about:
1. Apartment gardening?
2. Italian cooking?
3. Song-writing?
4. Deep-see fishing?
5. Healing crystal therapy?

Real examples
There are lots of examples available on the internet for you to look at; simply do a search for 'style guide'. There are also free Style Guides available. Ideally a Style Guide would be created specifically for your book so that it reinforces the topic you are writing about. If it seems unreasonable to create a different Style Guide for each book, it's still very worthwhile to create a general Style Guide that could be suitable for all your books.

Two ways you can apply a Style Guide to your book:
1. Template
With this method, the Style Guide is created then turned into a
Microsoft Word document with pre-selected colours, titles,
icons, fonts and sections ready for you to start writing directly
into. Even with this method it's still important to check that the
design and formatting are still correct after you finish writing
your book.

2. Reference
In this method, you ignore the formatting and design and start
writing the content of your book, including text and graphics.
After you complete the writing process, you would then
methodically and manually apply the design and formatting
rules from the Style Guide.

Combining design and formatting

In addition to formatting your layout, attention should be given
to the design of content in your book. While formatting deals
with layout, design is to do with the more intricate elements of
how things look. For example, a designer may select a limited
range of fonts for the titles, quotes and main body. The choice of
font can play a big part in the way information is perceived. For
example, the font 'Comic Sans' would hardly be appropriate for a
medical brochure about rectal examinations and we wouldn't
expect to see it on a tombstone. A designer may choose colour
combinations that create a theme which is sympathetic to the
book. Perhaps a careful combination of earthy greens and
browns for page titles could work well for a book about hiking.

In this book, after reading the first couple of chapters, you know that:

1. **The use of type fonts is the same** for all chapter titles, overviews and main content – there's a visual ease about how the written content flows and looks due to the consistency and white-space separation.

2. **Each chapter has a brief overview** under the title so readers can get a brief sense of the topic before they start reading. This gives them fore-warning of the upcoming information and helps put context around the content in previous chapters.

3. **Each section has a summary** so the reader gets the key points emphasised and reinforced. The summary also provides an easy way for readers to review the ideas later.

4. **The book has images** – at least one per chapter - which add clarity and a little humour to the message. Readers quickly build an expectation that further images are available to help explain concepts.

A consistent presentation and pleasing visual theme compliments the information and adds value to your book

Information Chunking

The method of Chunking simply means to separate sections of information in a way that makes it easier to read. In its simplest form, 'Chunking' can be using a sensible paragraph structure. When writers 'Chunk' their writing they remove the monotony of an endless sea of words and give clarity by separating different ideas.

A good method is to break your writing down into a new paragraph for each new sub-topic within the main topic. If you add a brief sub-heading in bold, then you provide further clarity for your readers. This is helpful because it emphasises aspects of the writing, making them more memorable. It also enables your readers to find particular information easily when reviewing the book.

Chunking is also powerful because it enables writers to emphasise content. When specific ideas are buried in large, un-paragraphed sections of writing, the impact can be lost. With Chunking, a writer can emphasise their message because of the white space created around that piece of information. Further impact can be achieved by reformatting into larger text like this:

Further impact can be achieved by using a big font with lots of white space around it

Book Formatting Tips

1. Use a limited range of fonts
Stick to one or two and use them consistently. For example, chapters may be in Franklin Gothic, bold, 24 pt, with the main body text in Cambria, 12 pt. Sub-titles could be in Cambria 14 pt, bold, while 'quotes' could be in Cambria, 26 pt, italic. In this example I use only two fonts while altering the size and style. Whatever font types and styles you choose, ensure that they are consistent throughout each chapter in your book.

2. Reference your graphics
Keep the size of your graphics (photos/diagrams/drawings) similar where possible. Align them consistently on the page, for example, all aligned to the left of the page. Give a reference and title to all graphics in your book and locate it in the exact same position (relative to the graphic) every time.

For example:

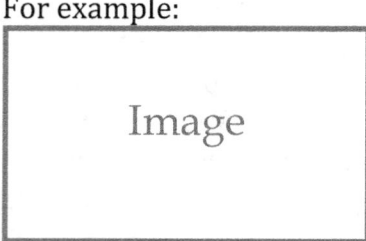

Image X: Energy variation in song sections

3. Ensure a consistent arrangement of content throughout your book
This refers to how you organise text and graphics on the page. For example, refer to any chapter in this book and you will see that it has a consistency with the position of text for titles, overviews and summaries. The order of content in each chapter is also consistent and looks like this:

Title > overview > author's note > detail > graphic > summary

Summary

1. Good formatting inspires reader confidence through visually appealing design and a professional arrangement of content.

2. It enables writers to add focus to the content by emphasising/de-emphasising the content.

3. Refer to other books to help you find a formatting style you like that you might adjust for re-use in your own books.

4. Keeping formatting in mind while writing can prompt writers to generate the right content e.g. author's notes, explanatory notes, quotes, examples.

5. Decide on your book's format early on as it guides you with the content you need to create.

Image F – Decide on your book's format early on

Theory and Application

Putting theory into practice gives meaning to the information you provide

Author's note:
Some years ago and for some time, I had been concerned at my tertiary students' level of understanding at the end of their course. The course was well planned, the content was concise, the delivery engaging and still their knowledge was lacking. It wasn't until a colleague made this brief comment, "the sooner I stop talking and get my students to do something, the better". His comment stuck and I immediately implemented it into my teaching: I cut my lecture delivery by 50% and replaced it with problem-based activities based on the lecture topic. "Take your new information and apply it to this problem", I told them. I never looked back: the 'learning by doing' principle worked almost overnight.

What is the theory and application principle?

When we write books that require our readers do something we need to link the knowledge with action. Doing this provides a way for readers to apply the information, making it more meaningful. This is because learning really happens when people apply the knowledge by doing something related. For example, someone can read a great book on learning to drive a car (theory part), but it won't be until they get into the car and try and drive it (action part) that they start to learn. It's at this point that the person is connecting knowledge with the application.

A good instructional book will include the knowledge and guide the readers on how to apply it. Such a book provides the reader with relevant knowledge at the appropriate level of complexity and in the right sequence. So often, books get the theory part right, leaving the reader reasonably well prepared, but miss the critical next step of showing them how and when to apply their new knowledge. A book that prepares the reader with the knowledge, then guides them on how to apply the theory provides the reader with a complete package of learning.

Practice without theory is blind,
theory without practice is empty

Paraphrased from Immanuel Kant: "Experience without theory is blind, but theory without experience is mere intellectual play"

Why the theory and application principle works

In academia, most agree that students learn best by doing. We call this, 'learning by doing'. It works because learners gain a deeper understanding when they have to take their new knowledge and do stuff. They make mistakes, they reflect on what worked and what didn't, and try again. They keep working on it until they get the desired results. When our readers apply the knowledge, the knowledge makes sense, has more meaning, and puts it into context with reality.

Being able to apply knowledge provides a reader with skills that can help develop new leisure pursuits and career opportunities. Helping your readers in this way can transform your book into a very valuable resource.

*A book that prepares the reader
with the knowledge, then guides them on
how to apply it, provides them with
a complete package*

How to use theory and application in your writing

When your goal is to have your readers do something related to the knowledge you need to think about:

1. The best activities to reinforce the knowledge.
2. Locating those activities at the appropriate place in your book.
3. Ensuring that the activities are explained well.
4. Ensuring the activities have a useful outcome that will benefit the reader.
5. Making sure the activities are at the right level of complexity.

When we write activities, we need to ensure that our readers are carefully guided.
This means:

1. Creating activities using step-by-step, numbered instructions (not simply writing our instructions in a paragraph format).
2. Writing 'waffle-free' instructions.
3. Providing images and graphics wherever possible to enhance the instructions.

Summary

1. Writers can write better books when they consider how their readers will apply their new knowledge.

2. Giving readers clear and unambiguous instructions about how to apply new knowledge makes the knowledge more useful and meaningful.

3. When writing the 'theory' part of your book, try and cover enough detail to prepare your readers for the 'application' part.

4. For the 'application' part of your book, create a range of simple and complex activities to cater for the experience level of all your readers.

Image G – Putting knowledge into practise

Examples

Use examples to add clarity and context to your writing

Author's note:
I've always found visual examples to be an incredibly effective way to reinforce and explain an idea. In my earlier days as an architectural designer my job was to explain complex construction assembly by doing drawings for builders. If my drawings weren't clear, construction couldn't happen! As an educator, finding examples to support the knowledge is helpful but finding the RIGHT examples is crucial!

Why use examples?

Context and meaning

Examples provide readers with context and meaning around the knowledge they're reading about. Examples can expand ideas and link theory with reality, showing your readers how the information relates to the real world. They provide a bridge between different knowledge topics, where the example describes a connection or relationship. Giving examples, especially when they're 'real life' examples, adds a relevancy to what you're writing about because the 'real life' element can provide supporting evidence for the statement. Whether the examples are written, graphic, audio or video, they provide readers with a way to enhance their understanding.

The Power of Graphics

Graphics are more than eye-candy for readers, they provide an effective way for readers to gain an understanding more quickly because they see the entire idea instantly. A study at the Minnesota University School of Management in 1986 showed that presenters who used visual aids were over 40% more effective in persuading students to take a desired course of action. Images provide a powerful way to strengthen the message and are particularly useful for readers who learn better with visual material.

The process of explaining something in writing is a linear-sequential medium of communication. It creates a monolithic channel of complex information. It's a bit like eating a meal one spoonful at a time, without seeing the entire plate of food. The imparting of complex knowledge in written form can be slow, elaborate, and confusing for some readers. This is due to the sheer number of words required and the sequence and construction of ideas required to 'frame up' an idea or concept. Even simple elements can have wordy descriptions which require more processing time than viewing an image.

Graphics have another powerful trait: they can invoke emotion that can make your information more memorable. When images portray sadness, anger, or humour (to name a few) they can enhance a reader's memory, deepening comprehension and retention of ideas.

Graphic Description	Written Description
	A square is a shape with four sides of equal length, with the angle of any two adjoining sides being 90 degrees.

Image: Example of a single element or simple idea

The above example shows that there is instant recognition and understanding with the graphic, whereas the description takes more time to read, assimilate and understand. If we consider the written description as our theory and the graphic as our supporting example, we have a very powerful way of enhancing the things we write about.

Consider making a cup of tea or driving a car. If a writer itemised every step in the correct sequence with an explanation of how and why, the process can be long and potentially confusing. However, if each of the descriptive steps is reinforced with a graphic, then the explanation is much clearer.

How to use examples effectively

The first consideration when creating examples is to decide:
1. The best medium (written, graphic, audio or video)
2. The best method (story, instruction, scenario, principles, knowledge)
3. The best fit (what is most appropriate for your intended audience?)

Whichever formats your examples take they must resonate with your readers and support their understanding. To achieve this requires you to understand their needs of your audience so that you can select the most effective types of examples. If your book is about music production your readers will almost certainly want audio examples. Younger readers may require lots of pictures. Repair and maintenance guides, even for advanced readers, will likely require a lot of images.

Using written examples

It's common for writers to make statements which leave readers wanting more information, for example:

It's important to paint the exterior of your house when the weather is not too hot.

While this is apparently good advice, the recommendation can leave the reader wanting to know more. This type of statement may generate further questions for a reader, like when *not* to paint the house. The reader may then want to know what you mean by 'exterior', and 'not too hot'. Let's try the statement again, using a very brief written example as part of the instruction:

It's important to paint the exterior walls of your house when the weather is not too hot. Painting on a cloudy day with a mild temperature of around 10 – 30 degrees Celsius works well. Painting when the weather is hotter than this can cause lack of paint adhesion later on.

Using Multi-media

Writers can provide web-links and include CD's and DVD's with their books. These formats open up many opportunities to add further value to your book. For example, if you write a book on how to fix an engine you might include a web link to a video activity related to a topic in your book.

Here are some further ideas for adding multi-media content to your book:

1. EBooks and electronic versions of the printed book

2. Audio book versions of the printed book

3. Audio and video interviews

4. Video reviews and 'how-to's'

5. Printable posters and diagrams

6. Image libraries

*Examples link theory with reality
and show your readers how the information
relates to the real world*

Summary

1. Get into the habit of giving examples to add context clarity to your statements.

2. Know your target audience and actively select the most effective style of example rather than defaulting to written examples.

3. Use graphic examples where possible, as studies show this to be an effective means of deepening understanding and improving knowledge retention.

Image H – Putting theory into context with examples

Validation

Be a credible writer: back up your claims with evidence

Author's note:
I'm particularly sensitive to this topic because as a lecturer
marking student work, my students regularly make statements,
fashioned as fact, that often lack authentication. This has led me to
be much more aware of conjecture and speculation in both my
own writing and that of other authors.

What is validation?

For writers, validation is about providing justification to the claims and statements made. When we validate a claim, we are effectively telling the reader whether it is a fact or whether it is our opinion. Validating a factual statement usually requires the writer to provide some evidence to support the statement. This might be in the form of survey, a study or some statistics. It's then useful to provide a reference so that the readers can look further into the supporting information. If the writer is simply stating an opinion then they need to write it in a way that does not lead readers to consider that it's fact.

As a writer, whenever you're about to make a claim ask yourself:

1. How do I know this is true?
2. Where is the evidence to support this?
3. Is this claim based on all of the facts or some of them?
4. Is this really just my own opinion?
5. If you need to include a piece of research or historical event to support your claim then do it; it makes for better, more authentic writing.

Authors need to differentiate between personal opinion and universally accepted fact

Why is validation important?

Writers weaken their message when they make claims, fashioned as fact, that lack evidence. Validating your claims with supporting evidence provides justification to what you're writing about. It prompts the reader to accept an idea, therefore adding credibility and authenticity to the overall message.

If readers are uncertain about the authenticity of the information they may question all of it. It's very easy for writers to speculate and generalise about the topics being explored. The non-fiction writer's job is to provide good quality, authentic and relevant information for their readers. They need to avoid conjecture (an opinion or conclusion based on incomplete information) unless it serves a valid purpose. For example, this may be done for humour or to explore public opinion on a matter.

Writers weaken their message when they make claims, fashioned as fact, that lack evidence

How to use validation successfully

Here are some examples that show how a statement can be more authentic when it is supported by evidence:

Example: un-validated claim
"Non-fiction books should have a word count of around 10 – 15,000 words".
The problem with this claim is that it doesn't explain to the reader why it's true; there's no evidence to support it. For example, is this universally accepted or is it a belief held by one large publishing organisation or the writer?

Example: validated claim – using research
"Non-fiction books should have a word count of around 10 – 15,000 words because research shows that this is the optimum length to hold a reader's attention.
In this revised claim, we've added a reason, which adds context and meaning to the statement. But is it the author's opinion? Or is it a unified belief or fact? Let's improve this with the next example.

"Non-fiction books should have a word count of around 10 – 15,000 words because this is the optimum length to hold a reader's attention. This was found in a 2012 survey of 2,190 readers conducted by the HearSay Institution in Australia".
As a reader we feel much more satisfied in believing this claim because it's backed up by research data. The writer can add further authenticity to this by providing a link or reference to the survey.
By the way, this claim is completely bogus and fabricated solely for this example.

Example: validated claims – using historical events
"Perfecting the art of distraction is an effective way of redirecting the course of events in any situation. John Blue, an Englishman from Surrey, successfully showed on numerous occasions how the artful redirection of the attention of 3 – 5-year olds improved their mood and disposition."

This validation is almost complete but lacks real evidence, for example an actual date/time/place but is still far more compelling than no evidence. If you wanted to add more weight you might try this:

"Perfecting the art of distraction is an effective way of redirecting the course of events in any situation. President Abraham Lincoln successfully proved this during the siege of Vicksburg in 1863, where he successfully distracted the Confederate Army at the Mississippi River, splitting them in two, weakening their defenses, and resulting in a resounding victory." *OK, another completely bogus claim but it shows how we can provide evidence of an historical event, along with dates and famous people, to support our claims.*

Avoid making lots of unsubstantiated claims unless you specifically state that they are the author's (your) opinion

Summary

1. Avoid conjecture, where you make claims based on incomplete information or hearsay.

2. Differentiate between your personal opinion, the opinions of others, and statements of fact.

3. Support your claims and statements of fact with evidence where possible, to add credibility to your message.

4. Claims are convincing when they are based on research or historical events.

Image I – Writers need to validate their statements for credibility

Keeping it Interesting

Keep your readers interested by using simple strategies to spice up your content

Author's note:

My experience over many years of writing is that <u>how</u> we present our content is as important as <u>what</u> that content is. Just like the delight you experience when you're served a well-presented meal at a great restaurant; it not only tastes great, but looks fantastic. In other words, how it looks affects how it tastes and this improves the dining experience. Some years back I experimented with different ways of presenting a topic of learning material. It was the same information, just presented differently and I wanted to know what my colleagues and students like the best. The favourite picks were always the ones that presented the information with variation and interest while maintaining a consistent theme. It became overwhelmingly clear that readers enjoyed well-presented material in favour of poorly presented.

What is it and why do it?

Page after page of text, void of variation can be a visual onslaught for our readers, due to the sheer volume and monotony of same-looking text. A visually monotonous presentation is acceptable for fiction, perhaps because readers don't want the presentation to distract them from the story. However, when we write books on non-fiction topics, adding a little visual spice makes the content more interesting, useful and memorable.

Providing visual variation creates an ongoing state of change which helps alleviate the tedium. When some of the content - like a summaries and quotes - appear different, they make it easy for readers to recognise and review that content later. Creating quotes from the most important statements in your book allows writers to emphasise important points that would otherwise be buried in the main body of detail.

Transitions

Creating interest and variation is a great method for transitioning between different topics. For example, writers can use a large quote of a salient point from their own writing at the end of each sub-topic within a chapter. Similarly, an image or diagram could be used to help further explain a complex idea.

Consistency

It's important that when we create variation, we also maintain consistency with the formatting. As discussed in the chapter on Formatting, consistency is important because it adds the perception of quality to the presentation. It allows readers to know in advance about upcoming content, like having a summary at the end of each chapter. So, while we aim to create reader interest through variety, we need to be consistent with our chosen method from chapter to chapter.

Font variation

Perhaps one of the simplest ways to create variation is to vary the font size of different types of content. The chapter heading, sub-heading, sub-topic titles and main body of text can all happily accommodate variation in the font. But consistency is important here; avoid using multiple different fonts and stick to one or two.

Ten tips on how to spice up your content
(these generally apply to each section/chapter)

1. Include at least one large quote of your most interesting statement for each section/chapter. Hopefully you've just noticed that this book uses this rule.

2. Use the TODS method to 'break up' the content (also used in this book).

3. Include at least one graphic for each section/chapter as a way to present your information in a visual way (sometimes used in this book). A graphical version of an idea is often very effective in reinforcing the written message.

4. Include questions at the end of each section/chapter to motivate your readers into thinking about your ideas.

5. Include an 'application' or 'practice' component at the end of each section/chapter to motivate your readers to do something with the information.

6. Include a cartoon or graphic that reinforces your message (ensure you have the rights to use it if you are not the original creator).

7. Use icons (small simple graphics) to support and reinforce titles and sub-titles. For example, use a cog wheel for complex information, a magnifying glass for the detail, a question mark for questions, and so on.

8. Use bullet points, numbered points and insets to create variation, but maintain consistency. In other words, if you use bullet points, duplicate the formatting throughout the book.

9. Use bold headings for each chapter.

10. Include an 'author personal comments' section or short-story at the start or end of each chapter. This can add a conversational tone and emphasise your own personal experience and opinion. It can work well if the bulk of your book is written in a more formal narrative style.

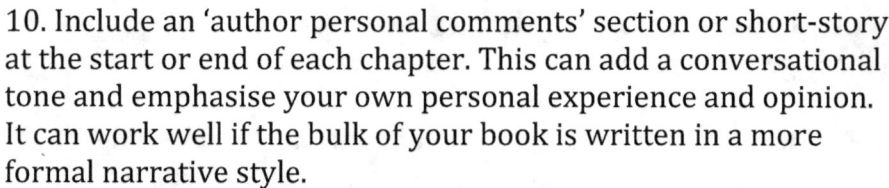

Include at least one large quote of your most interesting statement for each section/chapter

Summary

1. Add interest to your writing by providing variety in the visual presentation of your message.

2. Know your target audience and ensure the methods you choose add value and relevancy to the content. Avoid gimmicks.

3. Whatever you do, maintain consistency throughout your book.

4. Adding interest to the content is as much about 'how' it looks, as it is about 'what' the content is. Find ways to re-engineer the content into more meaningful ways for your readers (see the tips above).

5. Creating visual variation is an effective method for creating a transition between different topics and sub-topics.

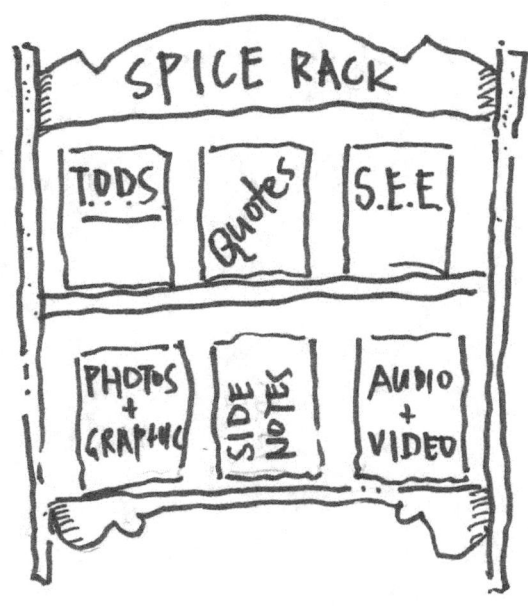

Image] What's in your spice rack.

Summarise

Sum up your chapter with a distillation of the key points so that readers know what's important

---

Author's note:
For a long time, summarising has been a fundamental method I've used for helping my readers and learners extract the important stuff from their reading. Early on in my lecturing career, I once had a student come to me after a four-hour lecture, confused and concerned that she didn't know what she had just learned. I asked her, "What are the three most important things that stood out for you"? After a moment's thought she told me, then we went on to discuss each of the three things. Within five minutes of summary and discussion she left smiling. From that moment on, I made a point to summarise every lecture presentation I did and include summaries in the learning material I created. My students, even to this day, thank me for it.

What is summarising?

Summarising is the method of condensing, emphasising, and simplifying the important points from a chunk of knowledge. It is a brief statement of the main points without all of the detail. When knowledge is summarised, it is shortened, simplified and refined, while retaining the essence of the original expanded version.

While a summary should be short and concise it should not include new content that wasn't in the original writing. The writer's intention should be to clarify and remind their readers about what's important.

A summary is a brief statement
of the main points without all of the detail

Why summaries are important for readers

Knowledge that is new and complex can quickly become 'inaccessible' for readers. They can easily lose the essence of an idea, particularly if the writer is interweaving interesting anecdotes, stories, and examples into their message. When a reader's attention is diminished it negatively impacts their ability to comprehend and retain the knowledge. The linear-sequential nature of writing (where only one idea can be expressed at any one time) can make the transmission of knowledge slow, complex and unwieldy. A summary allows writers to clarify and simplify the knowledge for their readers.

Summaries are an effective way for writers to add clarity to complex information by breaking information down into 'bite-size' chunks. This enables readers to relate the key points back to the complex knowledge they've just read.

A summary provides a quick and effective way to review the key points. Readers may find it useful after finishing the book, to go back and read the summary sections to solidify their thinking. They also provide a quick reference for later review. Locating the summary at the end of each chapter makes it easy for readers to find.

Summaries help readers build on their knowledge by assisting their comprehension of each chapter of a book before moving on to the next. In a book where each chapter introduces new knowledge which builds on the previous chapter, ensuring readers understand each chapter is vital to their overall understanding.

Simple and concise summaries help make complex information easier to remember. In this way, readers can use simple keywords and phrases to help trigger their memory about a particular topic.

Summarising enables readers to 'connect the dots' by putting context and meaning around a large array of complex information. A summary allows the reader to make sense of new and complex information and to walk away with a strong sense of what is important.

Highlighting the key points
helps readers make sense of one section
before they move on to the next

7 tips for effective summaries

1. The key point and explanation
This is a simple method of using a brief title, then following it up with a short explanation of a few lines or a very short paragraph. Remember that summaries by nature are short, concise and simple.
This item itself is an example, where the title is numbered, bold and on one line, with the short explanation below.

2. The key point
This is the method used in this book where a brief explanation is used without a title.

3. Use numbers or bullet points to emphasise
Always number your summary points as these create a reference for later use. It's much easier for a reader or author to refer to summary item number '3' in the Validation chapter than try and describe the summary. This is particularly useful if your book is intended as course material.

4. Keep them simple
The nature of a summary point is that it is short, simple and concise. It is a distilled version of the complex original.

5. Making them memorable
Writers may find it useful to include acronyms or memorable phrases that help readers to trigger the key points which remind them of the original complex idea. For example, "Every Good Boy Deserves Fruit" is a fun and simple phrase to remember EGBDF, the arrangement of musical notation. In this book, the acronym 'SEE' can be used for remembering Statement, Explanation, Example (refer to the chapter 'Crafting a Clear Message').

6. Ensure accuracy
The process of distilling complex theory and knowledge into simple ideas requires care and accuracy. Because a summary point is so short, it needs to be constructed carefully to ensure the essence of the original information is captured. Also, avoid adding new detail that wasn't in the original information.

7. Quoting
Summaries can be done using the method of quoting throughout the main body of text. Magazines and newspapers use this method and so does this book. The added bonus of this method is that strategic placement of the quotes can help add variety to the written content.

Summary

1. A summary is a brief statement or series of brief statements of the main points without all of the detail.

2. Summarising the key points helps readers correctly interpret the content by linking simple ideas to create complex knowledge.

3. A summary provides the reader with a quick and easy reference for later review.

4. Simplifying complex information into key points can make complex information easier to remember.

5. Ensure you correctly summarise the original information and avoid adding new information.

BEFORE   AFTER

Image K – Summarising helps your readers to join the dots

Check, Cheque, Chek

Consistent and error-free writing improves the quality and validity of your message

---

Author's note:
In my lecturing role teaching construction theory, I read A LOT of other people's written assignments and reflective practice. I'm continually amazed at one of the most consistent features of MOST of these submissions: an inability to run a grammar and spell-check. These types of checks are easy and relatively quick to do, yet without them they can significantly affect the quality of the information. There's nothing quite like the embarrassment of presenting oneself as a knowledge expert then jeopardising that position with writing errors. This is the one thing that made me very nervous about writing this book! While I've done my best to eliminate writing errors, I fully expect readers to find them and point them out. For your interest, I've re-written this book twice and had it proof-read and edited three times.

Why is checking so important?

Spelling, Punctuation and Grammar
The most obvious things to get right in any book are punctuation, spelling and grammar. Consistent errors in these three areas can bring into question author literacy, credibility and the quality of their message. High numbers of errors can be incredibly distracting for readers, and in worst cases, rendering a book confusing and unreadable.

It's not necessarily about making your book a literary masterpiece. At the very least, your non-fiction book needs to be free from errors that might irritate your readers and interrupt an otherwise clearly delivered message. Simple punctuation and spelling errors are easily fixed using the built-in automated functions of most word processing software. Even a misplaced comma can cause confusion with a written statement. The book titled, 'Eats, Shoots and Leaves' (Lynne Truss) humorously discusses how punctuation makes a difference. Just one erroneous comma in this sentence turns a bamboo-munching Panda into a gun-toting villain who enjoys a pre-felony snack. Similarly, a missed comma turns an innocent, "Let's eat, Mum", into "Let's eat Mum". Two sentences, one comma, totally different meanings.

Formatting
A good book needs a consistent visual arrangement of content from pages to chapters. This means being consistent with your font use for the chapter titles, overviews, detail, summaries and quotes. Maintaining consistency with vertical spacing between text elements is also important. However, formatting during writing is complex because you have to focus on two things simultaneously. A simple way to get around this is to write first and format later using a Style Guide. Doing this allows you to concentrate on the writing first without the added stress of trying to get the visual arrangement right. If you need a refresher on Style Guides, please review the 'Formatting' chapter.

Spelling and grammar errors can bring into question author literacy, credibility and quality of their message

Ways to check your content

1. Common word processing software (e.g. Microsoft Word) includes one-click spelling and grammar checks that can catch the bulk of spelling and grammar errors.

2. Have someone review and comment on your book once you have completed the spelling and grammar checks. If you can't find a family member or friend to do this, there are cheap and effective online options such as **www.elance.com**, **www.freelancer.com** and **www.fiverr.com**.

3. Employ a designer to check/edit your book's formatting so that there is consistency in the presentation. The websites mentioned above are good places to find experts in this area.

4. Employ a designer to create a Style Guide. A good Style Guide can be used as a design template for all your books.

5. Whatever checking methods you use, ensure you do it carefully and BEFORE you publish. A poorly written book can damage a writer's reputation!

The very last thing a writer needs is to have the communication medium affecting the transmission of knowledge

Summary

1. Check and correct spelling, grammar, and punctuation BEFORE you publish.

2. Use the built-in spellcheck features available in most word processing applications.

3. Take your time when error-checking and get it right BEFORE you publish.

4. Focus on getting the content created first THEN focus on correcting the errors.

Image L – Get serious about checking for errors before you publish!

Bringing It All Together

12 summary tips from this book

1. Top-down planning
Design with the end in mind: Identify the primary goal for your book and imagine it fully complete with all its features. Map out the topics of your book before you start writing.

2. Decide on your Outcomes
Outcomes provide clear goals for writers and clear expectations for readers. Construct a clear and concise set of outcomes and use these as your guiding light when writing.

3. 5 W's and an H
What, Why, Where, When, Who and How; a method for ensuring writers include all the important and relevant information about their subject matter.

4. Use a narrative style to suit your audience
Knowing your intended audience allows you to craft and pitch your message at the right level to suit their needs.

5. Craft a clear message
Structure your delivery of knowledge and information for ultimate clarity. Try using the TODS and SEE methods and include a glossary.

6. Format carefully
Organise your layout and content visually for maximum reader impact. Consider using a Style Guide as a template that can be used for many of your books.

7. Use theory and application

Putting theory into practice makes more meaning out of the information you provide. Always look for ways to get your readers to put theory into practice by including activities.

8. Give examples

Use examples to add clarity and context to your writing. They can be 'real life' or hypothetical but use them as much as you can.

9. Validate your statements

Add credibility and relevancy to your information by backing up your claims with evidence.

10. Keep it interesting

Add some spice to the content and formatting to stimulate reader interest and hold their attention.

11. Summarise the knowledge

Complete the chapters of your message with a distillation of its key points.

12. Check and check again

Error-free writing improves the quality and validity of your message, inspiring reader confidence in the knowledge.

Final Notes

Thanks for taking the time to read this book.
I sincerely hope it has given you ideas and inspired your
creativity with your non-fiction writing endeavours.

You're welcome to contact me to discuss any of the information
and ideas in this book – I answer all emails.

I would appreciate it greatly if you could take a few minutes to
leave me a review on Amazon.

Best wishes and kindest regards
Amos Clarke

Email me: show.pony@live.com

Other Books by Amos Clarke

Macro-Mixing for the Small Recording Studio
Produce better mixes, faster than ever using simple techniques that actually work

'Macro-Mixing for The Small Recording Studio' is intended for beginner and intermediate mixing engineers who want to find new ways to massively improve their workflow and the quality of their studio mixes. The book is packed with techniques, examples, guides, and tips to help you create a 'break-through' with your mixing. The author includes anecdotes from his own experience working with bands and working on mixing projects.

Available in print and kindle formats at www.amazon.com

56 Mix Tips for the Small Recording Studio
Practical techniques to take your mixes to the next level

Create magic in your mixes. Flip to any page, read the technique, and apply it. It's really that simple. This is not a book that trawls relentlessly through the world history of mixing before providing any useful advice. It simply gets straight into the business of giving you real tried and proven mixing tips that actually work. And there's plenty to keep you busy. The book covers processing such as compression, equalization, panning, parallel compression, transient manipulation, harmonic distortion, delay based effects and much more.

Available in print and kindle formats at www.amazon.com

Song Arrangement for the Small Recording Studio
Practical techniques to take your songs to the next level

Song Arrangement for the Small Recording Studio, explores professional techniques for crafting great sounding music productions that will keep your listeners wanting more. Transform your productions by manipulating Builds, Transitions, Hooks, Groove, Pace, Masking, Lead elements (and much more) in your songs. This book compares many of its techniques to popular radio hits so that you can 'see' them in action.

Available in print and kindle formats at www.amazon.com

36 Song Arrangement Tips for the Small Recording Studio
Practical arrangement techniques to take your songs to the next level

36 Song Arrangement Tips for the Small Recording Studio, is the perfect compilation of song arrangement tips and techniques that will help you create great music productions. This book has similar content to the author's other book, Song Arrangement for the Small Recording Studio, but is formatted into an easy-to-read, tips-based reference (with brand new techniques) that is a perfect studio companion for the song-writer, producer, and mixing engineer. Includes links to free online material.

Available in print and kindle formats at www.amazon.com

www.ingramcontent.com/pod-product-compliance
Lightning Source LLC
Chambersburg PA
CBHW071224280526
45787CB00002B/790